THE ULTIMATE ADVENTURE GUIDE TO REYKJAVIK ICELAND

THE ESSENTIAL TRAVEL GUIDE FOR A PERFECT VACATION

Alistair Prose

Copyright © 2022 **Alistair Prose**

Table of Contents

INTRODUCTION

Iceland has swiftly become one of the top tourism destinations in the world, but it still feels like a well-kept secret. Perhaps that's because of its magnificent natural beauty or the stretches of open terrain with nothing but Icelandic horses and occasional waterfalls to remind you that you aren't utterly alone. It is a land of natural beauty as well as vibrant local culture, hospitality, and a strong national pride in its history and mythology.

From the Blue Lagoon to the famed Skogafoss waterfall, Iceland's scenery is the stuff of legend—sometimes very literally, since many of its most well-known places have been immortalized in Viking mythology and classic literature. When you arrive, prepare to be overwhelmed by the splendor of nature; around every bend in the road is another vista so breathtaking it doesn't seem quite real.

Iceland appears to be both the end and the beginning of the world. With boiling mud, floating ice, and geothermal steam, Iceland's dynamic landscapes are a reminder of how natural forces molded our planet. Everywhere you go in Iceland, you feel pleasantly insignificant yet emotionally linked to the huge scenery.

Iceland is a destination where nature reigns supreme; find out how to make the most of your trip with our Iceland travel guide. Aside from the sophisticated and cosmopolitan capital, Reykjavik, population hubs are modest, with diminutive towns, fishing villages, farms, and minute hamlets scattered along the coastal outskirts. The center of the country, meanwhile, is a starkly stunning wilderness of ice fields, windswept highland plateaux, infertile lava and ash deserts, and the freezing immensity of Vatnajökull, Europe's largest glacier.

Chapter 1

Making Travel Plans to Iceland

A trip to Iceland is more difficult to plan than trips to many other places with its spectacular volcanoes, lava fields, fjords, beaches, and waterfalls, it's no wonder that visitor numbers to Iceland have skyrocketed in recent years.

But many tourists overlook how perilous this wild and lonely island can be.

Some take undue risks and end up needing to be rescued, which is placing strain on Iceland's volunteer rescue service. Visitors have even been hurt or killed after mishaps on glaciers, beaches, and cliffs.

This can be avoided, though, and there's no reason you can't enjoy a fantastic, incident-free trip by following these Iceland travel guidelines.

Step 1: Decide when to visit Iceland.

The time of year you visit Iceland will make a major difference in what you see and how you experience the country, as well as how busy the attractions are. We've come at different times of year and have experienced everything from frigid snow to beautiful sunny days. Iceland at different times of the year.

Winter Travel to Iceland

Running about from mid-October straight through to the end of April, winter is the least busy time in Iceland.

The closer to December you travel, the darker the days will be in mid-December, you'll get less than six hours of daylight! In March, you would get up to 12 hours of daylight.

That darkness is fantastic for seeing the Northern Lights, so if that's a crucial concern for your trip, winter is the time you should come.

Winter brings snowy landscapes and ice driving conditions (see our guide to driving in Iceland in winter), and some portions of the nation, notably the high ground, become unreachable for all but the most extreme off-road vehicles.

I would not be deterred from visiting Iceland in the winter. Temperatures rarely fall well below freezing, there are fewer visitors, and the wintery landscapes are lovely. Plus, the potential of witnessing the northern lights is alluring!

Visiting Iceland in the Fall and Spring

April, late September, and early October are about as close to fall and spring as you are allowed to come in Iceland.

These are effectively the shoulder months, with longer days than in winter, less likelihood of snow, and more routes and attractions likely to be completely open and accessible.

While it's not going to be overly hot, the winter chill won't be around, and you have a better chance of seeing greener vistas. It also won't be as busy as summer time; however, the longer days will reduce your opportunity to see the northern lights.

Visiting Iceland in Summer

Summer is the most popular time to visit Iceland; therefore, costs are likely to be higher, and sites more congested with visitors. Roads will be open across the country, making attractions more accessible, and a number of tours that were not available during the other months will be available.

The lengthy days imply that you aren't going to view the aurora borealis. The nation will nevertheless be beautifully green and lush, with vivid wildflowers lighting up the landscape if you visit when they're in bloom. Also, a fantastic time to watch wildlife.

Here are Fahrenheit lows and highs for each month:

January: 36°F to 28°F

February: 37°F to 28°F

March: 39°F to 30°F

April: 43°F to 34°F

May: 50°F to 39°F

June: 54°F to 45°F

July: 57°F to 48°F

August: 57°F to 46°F

September: 51°F to 43°F

October: 45°F to 37°F

November: 39°F to 32°F

December: 44°F to 32°F

Step 2: Determine the Type of Vacation You Want to Take in Iceland

There are various possibilities for how to travel in Iceland, which can be broadly described as follows:

A Self-Drive Trip

Normally our preferred mode of transportation, and a fantastic alternative in Iceland. A self-drive holiday includes leasing a car and then driving across Iceland under your own steam, staying in different areas, and sight-seeing depending on your preferences.

You have the flexibility to reschedule sites and activities if the weather is unfavorable, add or delete sights from your itinerary if you wish, and generally have the most control over your trip.

The disadvantage of a trip like this is that it can turn out to be a more expensive alternative than a group tour once you've considered all the expenditures for the rental car, lodging, fuel, and so on.

A group guided tour

If you want to have someone else drive while you enjoy the magnificent vistas, you might prefer to take a guided tour. These come in many varieties, from single-day excursions to multi-day adventures, and you can book both private tours and group tours.

For example, there are a number of single-day journeys from Reyjkavik that include the majority of the highlights of Iceland, such as the Golden Circle and the Snaefellsnes Peninsula.

Many travelers, especially those with only a few days to spare, base themselves in Reykjavik and then take a series of single-day excursions to destinations to visit landmarks like the Golden Circle and the Blue Lagoon, conduct a glacier trek, and view the Northern Lights.

Although you do need to be prepared to spend some time in a bus, it is remarkable how much you can see doing day trips from Reykjavik, then returning back to your hotel in the city each night!

The drawback is that you don't have the ability to stop as and when you want, and on a group tour in particular, obviously, you'll be with a number of other people.

Of course, this can be a terrific way to meet people and have a social side to your trip.

A private guided tour

A private tour can be the "best of both worlds," but these tend to end up being the most expensive option for a trip, so unless there is a very large group of people or money is no object, we'd suggest that either a self-drive trip or a group tour are going to be better values.

Passports for Public Transportation and Buses

There are other sightseeing bus companies that offer transportation rather than entire trips. You buy what they call a "bus passport," which is available for different durations and covers different regions of the nation.

Step 3: Choose a schedule for your Iceland trip.

Now that you've selected when and for how long you want to visit Iceland, you're going to want to arrange a schedule. Of course, once you've started putting a schedule together, you might realize you need even longer in this great country—and that's OK, of course!

1–4 days in Iceland

I would propose that on vacations of one to three days, you focus on the sights nearby and within a three- to four-hour drive of Reykjavik.

For example, a day excursion around the Golden Circle, a morning at the Blue Lagoon, a day trip along the south coast of Iceland to visit some of Iceland's most famous waterfalls, and possibly a day trip up to the Snaefellsnes Peninsula

These may all be easily done as either a day trip from Reykjavik or as part of a solo drive tour.

4–7 days in Iceland

Four to seven days provide you with loads of choice in Iceland.

My advice would be to explore from the Snaefellsnes Peninsula in the west all the way through to Jökulsárlón in the east, taking in attractions such as the Golden Circle, the Blue Lagoon, the tremendous waterfalls of the south coast, and the glacier region in the south-east.

These would be great as part of a self-drive tour, or you could join various single-day tours from the city.

7+ days in Iceland

With seven days to spare and assuming you're not traveling in the dead of winter, the Ring Road is the obvious choice.

You'll be able to view the major highlights of Iceland on this spectacular excursion around the country, with more photo opportunities than you can imagine. These are popular options and may be done either as a self-drive excursion like these or these or as part of a group tour like this.

Alternatively, you might truly tour from the east of the country down along the south coast and see everything from the highlights to the less-visited sights, really taking your time and taking it all in.

Now you should have an idea of when you're going to visit Iceland, how long you're going to spend in Iceland, and what sort of trip you're going to undertake in Iceland.

How to get there

The primary airport in Iceland is Keflavk International Airport, which is 30 miles (50 kilometers) southwest of Iceland's capital, Reykjavik. The complete list of airlines that fly into Keflavk can be found at isavia.is/en.

A frequent bus service operates from the airport to Reykjavik, which takes roughly 45 minutes. Car rental companies are located either in the arrival hall or in a separate facility a short shuttle bus ride away. A taxi service works 24 hours a day.

Chapter 2

Towns and Cities to know

Reykjavik: Vibrant, inviting, and magnificent, Reykjavik is the capital and most popular tourist destination in Iceland. It is the closest to the airport and some of Iceland's famous landmarks. It's easy to visit them, too; shuttle trips depart routinely from the city, and offers are given for more extensive packages.

Akureyri: Often referred to as the capital of North Iceland, Akureyri is a harbor town that's home to some of the most gratifying whale watching in the world, with many cruises assuring views in the summer. The Akureyri Botanical Garden, founded in 1912, is famed for its colorful vegetation and walking walkways. A perfect vacation for nature lovers, Akureyri also offers trips to neighboring natural treasures, including possibilities on horseback.

IIsavk: Hsavk is home to Hsavkurkirkja, a must-see wooden church erected in 1904 and a primary reason tourists visit Iceland. Visitors will also enjoy the town's cultural museums, such as the Hsavk Whale Museum. Whale-watching from Hsavk is lovely, with various species frequenting the bay.

Höfn: A fishing village in the southeast, Höfn is principally noted for its stunning views of the Vatnajökull glacier, the largest ice cap in Europe. Surrounded by shoals and beaches,

Höfn has also served as a filming location for a few James Bond and Tomb Raider movies, among others.

Vk Mrdal: Despite its small population of 300 people, Vk Mrdal (or simply Vk) remains one of the most popular Ring Road stops for visitors traveling the south coast sightseeing route.Two of Iceland's most famous waterfalls—Skógafoss and Seljalandsfoss—sit between Reykjavik and Vk, making the two-and-a-half hour journey more than worth it. On clear days, the Eyjafjallajökull and Mrdalsjökull glaciers may also be seen, but Vk's largest appeal is Reynisfjara, a black-sand beach and one of Iceland's most famous natural features.

Vestmannaeyjar: The islands of Vestmannaeyjar (or the Westman Islands) are reached by ferry—oor a bus and a ferry, if you opt to visit from Reykjavik. A volcanic archipelago with some of Iceland's most diverse species, the Westman Islands are a must-visit for anybody wanting to be at one with nature.

safjörur: Home to Iceland's popular musical festivals—tthe safjörur Rock Festival and Vi Djpi Music Festival—safjörur is a music lover's dream. Surrounded by panoramic panoramas, these events offer a really unique experience.

Iceland has an area of approximately 40,000 miles2 (103,000 km2), which is nearly the same as the state of Kentucky. The Ring Road, which essentially circumnavigates the country, is 828 miles (1,332 km) long and takes about 17 hours to drive.

Many of the most popular spots to visit in Iceland are spread out along the Ring Road, but the heart of the nation—the Highlands—contains some of the most magnificent scenery.

Here's a breakdown of each of the key regions in Iceland.

SOUTHWEST ICELAND & REYKJAVIK

Keflavik Airport is close to Reykjavik. It is in the southwest of the country. By far the largest settlement in Iceland, it is a lovely city with charming old streets, museums, and a huge harbor. It's a popular destination as a base to view loads of neighboring sights.

They include the Golden Circle (ingvellir, Geysir, and Gullfoss), as well as the Blue Lagoon, the Fagradalsfjall Volcano, and the hot river of Reykjadalur. Tours often depart from Reykjavik, including day trips to the spectacular beauty of Landmannalaugar or the valley of Thórsmörk in the Highlands.

SOUTHERN ICELAND & VK

Vk is a seaside village in the south of Iceland. Occupying an isolated site near the Mrdalsjökull Glacier, Vk has become a popular stop on the Ring Road as the only center within a 50-kilometer radius with services.

It's a wonderful base for visiting the Reynisfjara Black Sand Beach and the Dyrhólaey Peninsula, which is home to a colony of puffins. Two of the most popular waterfalls in Iceland, Skógafoss and Seljalandsfoss, are close, as is the renowned DC-3 plane wreck. Ice cave excursions or hiking tours to the Mrdalsjökull Glacier also depart from Vk.

It's easy to get there from Reykjavk, and with a terrific mix of waterfalls, animals, and glaciers, this should be on any trip lasting more than a few days.

SOUTHEAST ICELAND & HFON

Further east along the Ring Road, the huge glacier of Vatnajökull dominates the horizon. There is minimal civilization here, and accommodations book up rapidly. But the area features one of the largest ice caps in Europe (Vatnajokull), good hiking paths in the Skaftafell National Park, and the Jökulsárlón Glacier Lagoon.

Another notable attraction is Vestrahorn, where rough, steep peaks, including the famed Batman Mountain, meet the water. The main town in the region is Höfn, which is 3 hours and 30 minutes' journey from Vik.

This is an excellent spot for getting close to the frigid side of the land of fire and ice. Glacier climbs, ice caves, glacial lagoons, and some magnificent mountain scenery make the trek out worth it.

THE EASTFJORDS & SEYISFJORUR

Seyisfjörur is a delightful multicolored settlement in the east of Iceland and the most attractive location for seeing the East Fjords. It's magnificently located, surrounded by snow-capped mountains and waterfalls.

East Iceland is defined by stunning coasts, small fjords, and a slower, more local pace. Although it gets less visitation than the southwest, some of the prominent features include Hengifoss, one of the best waterfalls in Iceland, and the basalt columns of Stulagil Canyon.

Many hurry by this area too soon on the Ring Road, but the two stunning sites above make it worth at least one night on any longer Iceland trip.

HSAVIK, MVATN, & THE NORTH

Mvatn is a region in the country's center-north.It features a plethora of natural wonders like lava structures, a unique geothermal wasteland, and pseudo-craters.

An hour north of the main Mvatn location, the lovely seaside port of Hsavk is where whale-watching trips depart. Known as the Whale Capital of Iceland, up to 23 species of whale can be observed here, and sightings are nearly assured in the month of July. More details are in our guide to Myvatn.

This is a terrific spot for slowing down, spending a couple of days, and seeing all the varied attractions.

THE HIGHLANDS

The Iceland Highlands are a hilly region in the country's center that is only accessible in the summer (unless you take a super jeep tour).It is desolate, huge, and remote, but boasts some of the most stunning scenery anywhere in the world.

Landmannalaugar is one of the most accessible areas, with sweeping, colorful mountains set in a large caldera. The driving here is feasible, and it includes fantastic hiking.

Other highlights of the highlands include the stunning Thórsmörk valley, the steaming rusty-colored Kerlingarfjöll, and the volcanic craters and calderas near Askja.

The Highlands is a wonderful destination for individuals who prefer adventure and are happy to drive down gravel tracks in a 44. It needs a little more planning, but it's our favorite spot in Iceland. You may reward yourself for the extra work by visiting some of the most picturesque hot springs in Iceland.

THE WESTFJORDS & SAFJRUR

The main town in the Westfjords, a large peninsula in northwest Iceland, is Safjörur. It features a lovely high street and a respectable marine museum, but the charm of this neighborhood is its local vibe. Only 10% of visitors come here; therefore, this is a place to get to know the people.

Stretching out into the Atlantic Ocean, the Westfjords are a collection of craggy peninsulas and large mountains that comprise stunning but desolate scenery. It's home to one of the best bird-watching places in Europe, and there are several natural hot springs that feel remote and truly local.

There are tons of fantastic things to do in the Westfjords, but it's a long way to drive. First-timers with 10 days or fewer should save the region for a second visit.

WEST ICELAND & SNAEFELLSNES

The Snaefellsnes Peninsula is often regarded as a mini-Iceland. Here you'll find a big glacier, crimson craters, basalt columns, stunning coast roads, beautifully sculpted mountains, and one of the most photographed waterfalls in Iceland, Kirkjufellsfoss.

In my opinion, none of it is the best of what Iceland has to offer, and most of the region's attractiveness is due to its closeness to Reykjavk. Nonetheless, if you are short on time, it makes for a fantastic extension to a 3-day Reykjavk and Golden Circle itinerary..

VISIT BREIAVIK BEACH.

Breivik is a perfect illustration of the Icelandic coastline, replete with towering black cliffs, a serpentine stretch of gold sand, and just one red-roofed church. Even better, due to the bay's isolated location in the West Fjords, you'll usually have the bay to yourself.

It's the ideal spot for a stroll down the beach in the summer, and in the winter, you can curl up with a thermos of hot chocolate and watch the sun set.

TAKE A BATH IN GRETTISLAUG.

The history of Grettislaug, one of Iceland's many hot springs, may be the best. Outlaw hero Grettir reportedly plunged into this hot pool to warm up after swimming 7.5 km through icy waters and drawing some jeers from the local women for the effects on his extremities.

It doesn't matter if the legend is genuine or not; lying in the hot water with Tindastóll towering over you on one side and the open sea on the other will make you feel as strong as a Viking. You might be able to glimpse the Northern Lights from the hot spring if you stay until nightfall.

VIEW WHALES NEAR THE HSAVK COAST.

The welcoming town of Hsavk is located in the far north of Iceland, centered around its harbor and in the shadow of the enormous Hsavkurfjall. It's a charming location, especially in the summer when the mountain is green and the clean seas reflect the brightly painted wooden cottages and sailing ships, but the main draw is whale watching.

Although whale watching can be done from Reykjavik, the only place to see blue whales is from Hsavk.The likelihood of seeing orcas, minke whales, fin whales, sperm whales, and humpback whales in these seas increases your chances of seeing other cetaceans as well.

WANDER THROUGH FLAT, FLORAL FIELDS.

Iceland's landscape is wild, desolate, and surreal. however pastoral With fields filled with delicate flowers and breathtaking views across to the more spectacular West Fjords environment, the little farming island of Flatey offers a tranquil retreat.

Visitors can come here and enjoy several activities, such as strolling through buttercup fields, admiring the scenery, or taking a leisurely boat cruise, and not have to worry about anything else. Icelanders view it as a rural utopia.

PROTECT THE HEIMAEY PUFFINS

If you're looking for something to do in August, look no further than the island of Heimaey. Around this time, puffin chicks leave their nests to accompany their parents as they fly out to sea in search of food. Many of them, though, get lost and fly into Heimaey town, where the kind locals kindly gather the fluffy little sea birds and release them somewhere safe.

The town's children are leading the pleasant, friendly event, and if you can't grin when you see a cheerful youngster delicately picking up a lost puffling, your heart must be as hard as Heimaey's shoreline.

GO SNORKELING AND DIVING AT SILFRA.

Swimming between tectonic plates is a wonderfully strange experience available in Silfra. The geological rift, which separates the North American and Eurasian continental plates, is noted for its glacial waters, which are famously clear. Accessing this unique diving location without becoming too cold is made feasible by the use of a dry suit. One of the most distinctive things to do in Iceland is to explore the Silfra tectonic plates.

Chapter 4

Fun activities in Iceland

1. Go on a Game of Thrones tour.

The majority of the popular HBO series' scenes depicting the severe conditions north of the Wall were shot in Iceland. Get a behind-the-scenes look at this epic series by taking a guided tour of the shooting locations, which are available for either one day or many days. A day tour lasting eight hours costs 13,000 ISK.

2. Check out Thingvellir Park.

The North American and European continental shelf plates are being driven apart in this national park, which is also a UNESCO World Heritage site. It is also the original location of the longest-running parliament in history, which the Vikings held here for political sessions in the tenth century (you can actually scuba dive between the plates for 1,500 ISK) (you can actually scuba dive between the plates for 1,500 ISK). If you want to get some fresh air and move around, there are a number of paths near one of the main stops on the Golden Circle. If you want to camp here, there are also a few places to do that. Free entry is offered.

3. Swim in the Blue Lagoon.

It is undeniable that Iceland's most well-known geothermal pool is the nation's top tourist destination, even though I found the Mvatn baths to be a more tranquil and affordable alternative. There is nothing else like it in the entire globe, despite being crowded and pricey. The seawater that feeds this enormous, milky-blue spa is heated by a nearby geothermal plant and is mineral-rich. You'll feel as though you're in the twilight zone when the silvery towers of the plant, billowing clouds of steam, and people covered in white muck are added. The entrance fee is 6,400 ISK.

4. Take a walk on the Fimmvöruháls Trail.

Try the shorter (but just as gorgeous) Fimmvorduhals path if 55 kilometers is too much for you. This journey from rsmörk to Skógar can be completed in one day or split into two. You have two options: set up camp or reserve one of the mountain cabins situated along the path. Just remember that the cottages sell out quickly! Because of the trail's moderate difficulty, you should have sturdy footwear and be in decent physical condition. As the weather might abruptly change, be careful to have rain gear. If you don't camp, hiking is free. If you left your car in Rsmörk, you can take a bus from there back to Skógar for 8,000 ISK each way.

5. Go Fishing.

The fish of Iceland are well-known.

Fishing is hugely popular here and a significant component of Icelandic culture and food due to the abundance of salmon, trout, cod, and haddock. From Reykjavik, you can take fishing trips to farther-flung locations like the Westfjords. They are pretty much everywhere to be found! For a three-hour fishing expedition, budget about 14,000 ISK.

6.   Check out the Skaftafell Ice Cave.

Adventurers from all over the world visit Vatnajökull National Park to explore these stunning ice caves. The caverns are a component of the second-biggest ice cap in Europe, which is also the largest in the nation. They are only reachable during the winter. With an ax and crampons, you may explore this alien setting inside the caves on guided tours. Tours run for about 4 hours and begin at 18,700 ISK per person.

7.   Kirkjufell Mountain

This famous peak protrudes from the scenery in western Iceland, close to the small settlement of Grundarfjörur. A number of waterfalls surround this impressive peak. It's a beautiful location to see the northern lights if you travel there in the winter. One of Iceland's most often captured landscapes is the mountain; chances are you've seen it on Instagram.

8. Enroll in a class at the Icelandic Elf School.

There is a select minority of Icelanders who unequivocally reject the existence of elves, trolls, and hidden people, despite the fact that few locals genuinely profess to believe in these supernatural beings. Students and guests are taught about Icelandic folklore at the Icelandic Elf School. The "hidden folk" and the 13 various varieties of elves that the school thinks live in Iceland are topics of discussion. While visiting Reykjavik, this is undoubtedly one of the oddest attractions to see, which also makes it one of the best. The 7,737 ISK price may seem a bit steep, but it also includes a supper of pancakes and jam, tea, and chocolates to accompany the 3–4 hours of instruction!

9. Visit the Penis Museum.

The largest collection of penises and works of art with penis themes may be found in the Phallological Museum, sometimes referred to as the Penis Museum. The museum contains approximately 300 exhibits, including (supposedly) troll and whale penises! If you're not too shy, this tiny museum will teach you so much! It costs 2,500 ISK to enter.

10. Drive the Golden Circle Attractions Trail.

The 230 km (140 mi) long Golden Circle passes some of the most well-known attractions in the vicinity of Reykjavik, such as Gullfoss, Thingvellir, and Geysir/Strokkur. This is the principal route for visitors who are just staying for one or two days, and many tourist buses use this route. The Keri volcano crater, the Hverageri greenhouse hamlet, the

Skálholt church, and the Nesjavellir or Hellisheii geothermal power plant are among the additional stops. Start your day early if you have a car to beat the buses. The entire trip may be driven in a few hours.

Chapter 5

How long should you stay in Iceland?

It's no secret that Iceland has quickly risen to the top of every traveler's wish list. This northern wonderland features some of the most spectacular scenery in the northern hemisphere, including glaciers, volcanoes, and ice caves, compelling visitors to return for more. Iceland has something for everyone, whether you want a quick getaway or a full backpacking adventure. However, before you pack your bags and head north, here are a few different itineraries to help you plan the perfect-length Icelandic vacation.

It is recommended that you spend at least 3–4 days in Iceland if this is your first visit. This is not enough time to explore everything the island has to offer, but it will help you plan a beginner's trip around the island. There's also a fantastic Icelandic road trip for those who want to tackle Iceland's famous ring road. The entire journey takes 24 hours; however, 7-8 days would allow you to visit all of the major stops along the way. In general, I recommend visiting Iceland for at least 7-8 days so that you have enough time to explore many of the tours and attractions in Iceland and Reykjavik.

Please see below for some good Iceland itineraries of 4 days, 6 days, and 8 days.

3 nights and 4 days of adventure in the winter

Iceland's capital and largest city is Reykjavik.

The view of Reykjavik from the top of Hallgrimskirkja church

Spend four days and three nights in Reykjavik, Iceland's capital city. This is an ideal location to visit during the winter to enjoy this winter wonderland.

Day 1: Fly to Keflavik Airport and then to Reykjavik. Spend the day visiting museums, galleries, spas, thermal pools, and boutiques. Because the city is small, you should be able to walk to all of these locations.

Day 2: Take a small walking tour with a group guide to see the landmarks of downtown Reykjavik on the second day of your trip. Don't miss Hallgrimskirkja, a well-known landmark in Reykjavik.

If the weather permits, take a tour outside in the evening to see the northern lights.

Day 3: On your third day of vacation, take a Golden Circle tour. On this tour, you will see a glacial waterfall (Gullfoss), the Great Geysir geothermal region with regular eruptions, and finally, Ingvellir National Park, the site of Iceland's first parliament.

Day 4: On your final day, unwind at the Blue Lagoon, a geothermal spa. Then, once you've recovered sufficiently, you can board your flight back home.

6 days and 5 nights of nature and city adventure

Spend six days and five nights exploring both the city and the great outdoors in Iceland. On this trip, you can visit shops and museums and see wildlife, geysers, and waterfalls.

Day 1: Upon arrival at the airport and subsequent transportation to Reykjavik, explore the city by visiting museums, naturally heated pools, restaurants, and nightclubs.

Day 2: Take a two-hour tour of the capital city with a tour group. The tour will take you to the city's highlights as well as historic landmarks. There are also a variety of interesting activities going on in the city, which you will learn about during the tour.

Day 3: On the third day of your trip, you will visit the Golden Circle. You will see a glacier waterfall and numerous geysers here.

Day 4: On your fourth day, go to the Blue Lagoon spa to relax in naturally heated seawater. There are saunas, steam baths, and various treatments available to assist you in unwinding and relaxing.

Day 5: Spend the fifth day exploring the south coast. The Seljalandsfoss waterfall, which is forty meters high, can be seen from here. The Sólheimajökull glacier will then be visible. The final stop will be a black sand beach and the Skógafoss waterfall.

Day 6: On your final day before flying, consider visiting the Reykjanes peninsula for another breathtaking view to remember.

Southern and Western Iceland in 8 Days and 7 Nights

This eight-day, seven-night tour takes you through Iceland's countryside. The trip will begin and end in Reykjavik, and you will have the opportunity to see beautiful glaciers, waterfalls, and the famous Golden Circle.

Day 1: Upon arrival at Keflavik Airport, a driver will transport you to your hotel in Reykjavik. Then, after a long day of traveling, you can spend the day relaxing or exploring the city. You will spend the night in Reykjavik.

Day 2: You will rent a car and drive around the historic Borgarfjörur area. With a stop at the Icelandic Settlement

Center, you can learn about Iceland's history. Then, visit the Hraunfossar and Barnafoss waterfalls. Then there are the Vgelmir and Surtseyli caves to see. Finally, your final stop of the day should be to see a man-made ice cave carved out of a glacier. You will spend the night in the Borgarfjörur area.

Day 3: On the third day of your Iceland vacation, drive to the Snaefellsjökull peninsula and see the Snfellsjökull glacier. This glacier is thought to be one of the Earth's seven energy centers. Along with the glacier, you'll see Dritvk Cove, some impressive cliffs, and a fishing village. You'll spend another night in the Borgarfjörur area.

The Golden Circle is one of Iceland's most popular attractions. This route will take you to Thingvellir National Park, where you can walk in a rift valley formed by the Eurasian and North American plates. You will then proceed to the Haukadalur geothermal area, where you will see a geyser spout. Finally, at the end of the day, pay a visit to the Gullfoss waterfall for a breathtaking view. Then, spend the night in Selfoss.

Day 5: The adventure today begins with a visit to the Seljalandsfoss waterfall, which you can actually walk behind. Following that, you can see the impressive Skógafoss waterfall. Then visit the Skogar Folk Museum and the black volcanic beach at Vk. If you want even more adventure and don't mind driving a little further, you should visit Skaftafell and the Jökulsárlón glacier lagoon. The extra driving time is well worth it. You will spend the night in the Selfoss area once more.

Day 6: Spend more time in the Selfoss area on the sixth day. Only this time, you should look into fun activities such as snorkeling or river rafting. Then you can go for a hike near Hverageri. You'll be spending the night here once more.

Day 7: Today you must return to Reykjavik. However, the journey does not have to be monotonous! Take the Hells Canyon route, and you'll end up inside a volcano. Then, make your way to Hverageri to explore the geothermal features that can be found there. You will spend the night in Reykjavik.

Day 8: To avoid overdoing it on your final day in Iceland, take a relaxing stroll through the capital city. Visit a local cafe, mingle with the locals, and snap a few more breathtaking photos before returning home.

Regardless of how long you stay in Iceland, you will have a fantastic time and see some of the world's most breathtaking sights. This Nordic island nation has something for everyone, and you will undoubtedly return home refreshed and content.

Chapter 6

What Should I Wear to Iceland?

Iceland always necessitates warm, very warm clothing that is suitable for walking and being outdoors. I've divided the types of clothing needed by season, including shoes. My advice is to always keep a spare pair of socks in your backpack, and if possible, bring two pairs of gloves in case one gets wet for any reason.

What should you wear in Iceland in the winter?

If you visit Iceland during the winter, you will need:

Thermal wind jacket with multiple pockets

Hiking boots that are waterproof

Winter boots

Socks made of thermal material

Gloves, scarf, neck warmer, and hat (fleece or technical fabric)

Trousers for skiing

Sweatshirt in fleece

Thermal shirts with long sleeves

Thermal leggings (for women), hiking pants (for men).

Swimsuit (beach or pool)

Hair conditioner or a good shampoo (the Icelandic spa's water is very sulphurous and will dry your hair).

Body lotion (for the same reason as above)

What Should You Wear in Iceland in Spring?

If you plan to visit Iceland in the spring, you will need:

Thermoplastic Raincoat

Hiking boots that are waterproof

Sneakers

socks made of thermal material

Gloves, scarf, neck warmer, and hat (fleece or technical fabric)

Sweatshirt in fleece

Thermal shirts with long sleeves

Shirts with short sleeves

Thermal leggings (for women), hiking pants (for men).

Swimsuit (beach or pool)

Hair conditioner or a good shampoo (the Icelandic spa's water is very sulphurous and will dry your hair).

Body lotion (for the same reason as above)

What to Wear in Iceland During the Summer

If you visit Iceland during the summer, you will need:

Jacket that is resistant to water

Hiking boots (ideally waterproof, but not required)

Sneakers

Socks made of thermal material

Hat, scarf, and warmer

Sweatshirts

Shirts with short sleeves

Leggings (for women), hiking pants (if you are a man)

In the event of exceptionally fine weather, shorts

Swimsuit (beach or pool)

Hair conditioner or a good shampoo (the Icelandic spa's water is very sulphurous and will dry your hair).

Body lotion (for the same reason as above)

What to Wear in Iceland in the Fall

If you plan to visit Iceland in the autumn, you will need:

Thermal wind jacket with multiple pockets

Hiking boots that are waterproof

Winter boots

socks made of thermal material

Gloves, scarf, neck warmer, and hat (fleece or technical fabric)

Fleece Sweatshirt Ski Pants

Thermal shirts with long sleeves

Leggings (for women), hiking pants (if you are a man)

Swimsuit (beach or pool)

Hair conditioner or a good shampoo (the Icelandic spa's water is very sulphurous and will dry your hair).

Body lotion (for the same reason as above)

Is it necessary for me to bring medicine to Iceland?

Yes, you should bring some drugs and medicines with you because it may be difficult to find a pharmacy.

Antipyretics (like Tylenol)

Anti-inflammatories (such as aspirin) (such as aspirin).

Antihistamines if you have allergies and/or antihistamine ointment

Medications for stomach problems (such as Imodium)

Muscle pain creams

Sunscreen (if it's sunny, even if you don't feel it)

Patches

insect repellents

Lip balm for medical purposes (to treat chapped lips)

Hand Cream for Medical Purposes (to be used on chapped hands).

Chapter 7

Iceland's Best Hotel

Hotel Icelandair Reykjavik Marina

Address: Mrargata 2, 101, Reykjavik, Iceland

Phone: +354 444 4000

Icelandair Hotel Reykjavik Marina is the country's premier hotel, owned and operated by Icelandair. The hotel is colorful, comfortable, and centrally located, and it is decorated in modern Icelandic style with unique references to the country's maritime history. Do you want to see an Icelandic film? They are shown with English subtitles in the attached Slipp Cinema. Hungry? Slippbarinn, the hotel's cafe and bar, serves a wide selection of local and international favorites. On the hotel's website or at the front desk, you can also book day tours to nearby landmarks.

Hotel Laxá

Phone: +354 464 1900

Address: Olnbogaás, 660 Mvatn, Iceland

Hotel Laxá is an excellent choice for an overnight stay if you are visiting Lake Mvatn and the surrounding area. The property is decorated in a clean, comfortable Nordic style, and it includes an attached restaurant serving delicious cuisine inspired by traditional Icelandic recipes. It's easy to spend more than a day or two in Mvatn, with day tours to nearby hot springs and lava fields, and Hotel Laxá will look after you while you do.

Hotel Kea

Address: Hafnarstraeti 87–89 in Akureyri, Iceland.

Phone: +354 460-2000

Hotel Kea has prime real estate in the heart of Akureyri, right next to the famous Church of Akureyri. It, like most hotels in Iceland, is happy to assist you in booking day tours to nearby areas. Akureyri is well-known for whale watching and horseback riding tours, as well as its proximity to the stunning Goafoss waterfall (or "Waterfall of the Gods"). The hotel is also decorated with an emphasis on elegance and comfort, providing a welcome respite after a day of adventure.

Hotel: Hverfisgata 10

Address: 101 Reykjavik, Iceland

Phone: +354 580-0101

The 101 Hotel is well-known for its luxurious spa and chic design, which incorporates an industrial aesthetic with clean minimalism. The rooms in this hotel range from doubles to full apartment suites. From the front desk, you can also book a variety of day tours. The 101 Hotel frequently offers deals and packages, so it's worth checking the website before making a reservation

Hotel Ion Adventure

Phone: +354 578 3720

Address: Nesjavellir vi Thingvallavatn, 801 Selfoss, Iceland

If you want to immerse yourself in the natural beauty of the area, the Ion Adventure Hotel is an excellent choice. The Ion Adventure Hotel, which is comfortable and equipped with a natural spa, including a sauna and outdoor hot pool, focuses on — you guessed it — adventures, with several unique tours on offer.

Hotel Rangá

Address: 851 Hella, Iceland

Do you want to spend the night at the foot of a volcano? You, of course, do. Hotel Rangá has such a unique location that it is almost always booked during peak season, and if you stay here, you will almost certainly see one of the many weddings held each year. The available tours at Hotel Rangá highlight the beauty of the stars and northern lights, as well as the luxurious experience of geothermal baths. But if you prefer hiking or kayaking, Hotel Rangá is also in a great location for all kinds of outdoor activities.

Hotel Katla

Phone: +354 487 1208

Address: Höfabrekka, 871 Vk, Iceland

Hotel Katla, which is owned by the same hotel company as Hotel Kea, is decorated similarly and offers many of the same amenities as its northern cousin. You won't find a better hotel to spend your nights in if your trip is focused on the beauty of southern Iceland.Reynisfjara black-sand beach, Skógafoss waterfall, Mrdalsjökull glacier, Vatnajökull National Park, and Jökulsárlón glacier lagoon are all within easy reach of Hotel Katla.

Hotel Frost and Fire

+354 483 4959

Address: Hverhamar, 810 Hveragerdi, Iceland

Frost & Fire, with a name as dramatic as the surrounding landscape, offers an off-the-grid experience 40 minutes from Reykjavik. The hotel takes pride in providing a resort experience, which includes geothermal swimming, an excellent restaurant, and luxuriously appointed rooms. Of course, there are numerous and beautiful sightseeing opportunities near Frost & Fire.

Hotel Egilsen

Address: Aalgötu 2, 340 Stykkishólmur, Iceland

Phone: +354 554 7700

Hotel Egilsen was once a farmhouse and retains all of its rustic charm. Hotel Egilsen provides a one-of-a-kind experience with cozy rooms, freshly prepared daily meals and snacks, and live storytelling in the common areas.

Best Restaurants

Rub23

Address: Kaupvangsstrti 6, 600 Akureyri, Iceland

Phone: +354 462 2223

Rub23 is a popular restaurant in Akureyri, serving seafood, sushi, and meat dishes. The lunch buffet is available every day, and the service is excellent. The restaurant also makes its own spice blend, which gives each dish a distinct flavor you won't find anywhere else.

Tryggvagata 1

101 Reykjavik, Iceland is the address for Bjarins Beztu Pylsur.

"Hot dogs," in two words. These aren't just any hot dogs; this Reykjavik stand is famous for its unique hot dog blend (beef, pork, and lamb) and fixings. It's open until 1 a.m., so if you've been drinking at one of Reykjavik's many pubs, end your night with one of the best hot dogs you've ever had.

Vesturgata 2a, Grófartorg,

101 Reykjavik, Iceland is the address of The Fish Company.

Fish Company is located in the Zimsen House, a former store built in the nineteenth century, and is both modern and cozy—aa style that is reflected in the menu. Chef Lárus Gunnar Jónasson serves fresh seafood with a modern twist on traditional recipes.

Grillmarkau's

phone number +354 571 7777.

Address: Lkjargata 2a, 101, Reykjavik, Iceland

Grillmarkau, which uses meat and produce from local farmers, is an excellent choice for visitors who dislike seafood. The seasonal menu focuses on infusing dishes with distinct flavors imparted by smoke, wood, and coal.

Forrétta Barinn Courtesy of Forrétta Barinn

Address: Nlendugata 14, 101 Reykjavik, Iceland

Phone: +354 517 1800

Forrettabarinn is an excellent, low-cost option for any meal of the day. It is delicious, popular with locals, and comfortably decorated in a modern diner style. It's best known for its four-course menus, which will fill you up without emptying your wallet.

Suur-Vik

Address: Suurvegur 1, 870 Vk, Iceland

Phone: +354 487 1515

For good reason, this is one of VK's most popular restaurants. Restaurant Suur-Vik is a must-stop for lunch or dinner if you're touring Iceland's south coast or black-sand beaches. The menu features hearty, locally sourced fare, as well as gluten-free and vegan options.

Salka Restaurant

Phone: +354 464 2551

Address: Gardarsbraut 6, 640 Husavik, Iceland

After some whale watching, head to Salka Restaurant for a pizza or the day's catch. It's popular with both tourists and locals, and it's also a great place for groups larger than 15. In fact, there is a menu specifically designed for large groups.

The Best Shopping

There are boutique shops, locally owned cafes, craft stores, and the like everywhere in Iceland, but here's what's best in Reykjavik.

Laugavegur

Laugavegur, Reykjavik's main street, is lined with fun shops. Local boutiques, cute and delicious cafes, vintage stores, book stores, and the flagship location of 66°North can all be found here. In other words, if you want to go shopping during your trip, Laugavegur should be your first stop.

Kolaporti

Phone number: +354 562 5030

Tryggvagötu 19, Old Harbour Grófin, Reykjavik, Iceland.

The Kolaporti flea market is located near the Reykjavik Art Museum and the world-famous hot dog stand Baejarins Beztu Pylsur. It is an unassuming building, with a line of people usually heading in. This weekend-only shopping experience includes booths selling old and new items, a food court, and stalls manned by locals looking to get rid of some of their clutter. The flea market has a stoop sale feel to it, and you might even come across a real treasure.

Fr Lauga's

phone number +354 534 7165.

Address: Laugalkur 6, Reykjavik, Iceland (105).

Fr. Lauga (or Mrs. Lauga), a market that stocks mainland imports, is a great stop if you're craving fresh fruit or want to try the kombucha bar. If you've chosen to stay at an Airbnb during your trip, pick up some snacks for the day or stock your kitchen.

Lucky Records

Address: Rauarárstgur 10, 105 Reykjavk, Iceland.

Phone: +354 551-1195

Lucky Records began in 2005 as part of the Kolaporti flea market and has since grown to become Iceland's largest record store, stocking a massive selection of new and used vinyl and CDs. Expect a diverse selection of genres, including Icelandic music, as well as T-shirts, posters, and other mementos.

Herrafataverzlun Kormáks og Skjaldar

Phone: +354 511 1817 Laugavegur 59, Basement 101, Reykjavik, Iceland

This men's clothing store takes pride in its beautiful aesthetic and finely crafted clothing. It's worth a visit if you're interested in Icelandic fashion or looking for a gift for someone special. It's known for its military-adjacent style and wide range of offerings.

Chapter 8

What You Need to Know About Iceland Visas

You may need to apply for a visa to visit Iceland, depending on where you are traveling from.

Iceland is not a member of the European Union (EU), but it is a member of Schengen, a treaty between 26 countries that allows its citizens to travel visa-free among them. Austria, Belgium, the Czech Republic, Denmark, Estonia, Finland, France, Germany, Greece, Hungary, Iceland, Italy, Latvia, Liechtenstein, Lithuania, Luxembourg, Malta, the Netherlands, Norway, Poland, Portugal, Slovakia, Slovenia, Spain, Sweden, and Switzerland are all part of the Schengen area.

Passport holders from a number of countries outside the Schengen area can also visit Iceland without a visa. Australia, Ireland, Israel, Japan, New Zealand, the United Kingdom, and the United States are among the countries whose citizens can stay in Iceland for up to 90 days in a 6-month period. A valid passport or relevant travel document valid for at least three months beyond your intended stay is required.

Other nationals must apply for a short-stay Schengen visa (or C-visa) before visiting Iceland or the rest of the Schengen area. The visa permits a maximum stay of 90 days in any six-month period. Tourists, business trips, family visits, official visits, and short-term studies are all eligible for such visas.

You can apply for a short-stay C-visa at embassies and consulates around the world in the cities listed on the Icelandic Directorate of Immigration's website (UTL). Many embassies and consulates use third-party service providers to receive applications. Individuals who have been granted a residence permit in Iceland but need a visa to enter the country must apply for a D-visa.

Visas for most countries' nationals cost €80 (approximately US$95) for adults and €40 (approximately US$46) for children aged 6 to 12. (There is no charge for children under 6 years.) Although visa processing usually takes no more than 15 days, it can take longer. As a result, you should apply for your visa at least three weeks in advance. Before applying, double-check the full list of requirements, which may include things like proof of travel medical insurance and financial means, with the consulate, embassy, or service provider.

Visas can only be extended for more than 90 days in exceptional cases. Extension applications can be submitted to the Icelandic Directorate of Immigration in Reykjavik. Under certain conditions, multi-entry visas allowing for repeated 90-day stays in the Schengen area in each 180-day period of up to 5 years can be granted.

Working holiday permits for Iceland are only available to Japanese nationals who live in Japan and are between the ages of 18 and 26. The permit is only valid for one year. Visit the Directorate of Immigration's website for more information on working holiday permits. Other nationals and those planning to work for an extended period of time will need to apply for a work-based residence permit.

Before traveling to Iceland, residents of the European Union should obtain a free European Health Insurance Card (EHIC). This entitles you to free medical care if you need it while you're away. The EHIC, however, is not a replacement for travel insurance, which you will still require if you require non-urgent treatment, ongoing care, or repatriation.

Travel insurance is not required if you live in the United States, but it is highly recommended. It's a good idea to have some travel insurance in case of weather or volcanic eruptions. Furthermore, your US health insurance plan is unlikely to cover you in Iceland.

Chapter 9

13 Things You Should Know Before Visiting Iceland

The number of visitors to small, ravishingly beautiful Iceland is on the rise, but this small country wasn't always so crowded with tourists, and there are several important things to know before you go.

Travelers who are considerate of local etiquette will want to minimize their impact on the pristine environment. Small mistakes in these wild landscapes can result in life-threatening situations for both the visitor and the search and rescue operations that are mounted to save them. This helpful guide can assist first-time visitors in avoiding social embarrassment, traveling responsibly, and having a safe and informed trip.

Recognize the impact of tourism on Iceland.

Iceland has a population of approximately 366,000 people. Most Icelandic sights, from the thundering waterfall Skógafoss and basalt beach Reynisfjara to the wild interiors at Landmannalaugar and órsmörk, had no need for large car parks, safety placards, or hordes of park rangers before travelers began arriving in droves (with numbers that topped 2 million per year prior to the pandemic). Creating an infrastructure capable of accommodating its grateful new visitors while preserving the untouched feel of one of the world's most unique landscapes has been a major challenge for Iceland.

Use your common sense.

Some tourists have acted foolishly in Iceland's breathtaking landscapes. Visitors in sneakers and light jackets walk onto the Sólheimajökull glacier; a family tries to drive across the Langjökull glacier in a small SUV; a teenager bravely jumps into 2°C (35°F) waters at ingvellir National Park; and tourists are sucked into the waves at black-sand Djpalónssandur beach.

Despite Iceland's treacherous terrain, there are no guardrails along cliff edges and no ropes alongside cascading waterfalls. Icelanders would rather not mar their natural beauty with obvious signs or railings and instead rely on visitors to be cautious. And if there are warning signs or barriers, follow them.

Hiking requires appropriate attire and outdoor gear.

Bring good maps, appropriate equipment, and, as you've heard before, common sense. Check out a hiking or cold-weather packing list. Consider this: if you didn't have access to a car or a building, would you be warm and dry in what you were wearing? No hiking in jeans, no glacier climbing without proper guidance, no river fording in subcompact cars, and no camping without hard-core waterproof tents. Then simply relax and take in all of the beauty; no fear is required.

Being prepared can allow you to visit beautiful wilderness areas like the Westfjords' Hornstrandir Nature Reserve, which is known for its Arctic foxes, spectacular birding cliffs, and unspoiled hiking and camping.

If you need additional equipment while in Iceland, Reykjavik has a plethora of suppliers, including Fjallakofinn.

Plan ahead of time when hitting the road or hiking trails.

Having your own wheels in Iceland is a wonderful treat because it allows you to explore the vast landscape at your leisure. Always plan ahead of time by researching driving times and road conditions (via the Icelandic Road Administration), weather forecasts, safety concerns, and, if hiking, trail conditions and requirements. Inquire with locals, who will be familiar with the traps and pitfalls of each location. Then pay attention. Make a schedule that works for you. You don't want to be stranded on a hillside in fog or sleet (on foot or in your car) with no food or water and no idea how to return to humanity.

Safe Travel is an ICE-SAR (Icelandic Search and Rescue) website that provides travel and weather alerts and information, as well as a smartphone app (useful in an emergency) and procedures for filing a travel plan.

Ferafélag slands (the Icelandic Touring Association), which operates many huts, campgrounds, and hiking trails, is another good source of information.

Off-road driving is not permitted.

Never go off-road. It's illegal and extremely harmful to the environment. Cavalier tourists leave tracks where they've broken the rules, enticing others to do the same. Even if you have a 4WD, stay on marked roads.

Before swimming in hot springs, always shower with soap.

The excellent natural hot springs you'll find from the town center to the fjord side are part of Iceland's unique gift. Going to the local hotpot to soak and gossip is practically a national pastime. It is, however, an absolute hygiene and etiquette requirement to thoroughly wash with soap before donning your swimsuit and entering the hot springs and pools. Because most pools are not chemically treated, cleanliness is an important consideration. There's no faster way to disgust an Icelander than to jump in dirty water, whether you're at the famous Blue Lagoon or the remote Krossnes Lagoon. As you enter the changing room, remove your shoes and place them on the rack provided.

Tour the more remote or dangerous landscapes.

The tour operators in Iceland are professional and knowledgeable, and they can take you out into the rugged country by super-jeep, amphibious bus, snowmobile, helicopter, and other means. A tour can provide insights and guidance through dangerous landscapes that you should not attempt alone.

When driving, stay on designated roads.

Understand which roads are accessible in the vehicle you're driving. Beyond Iceland's main Ring Road (Route 1), fingers of sealed road or gravel extend out to most communities, until you reach the F Roads, which are bumpy tracks only passable by 4WD. F roads are extremely dangerous for small cars. Traveling on them in a rented 2WD voids your insurance. Avoid it, or hire a 4WD or go on a 4WD bus or super-Jeep tour. Similarly, attempting to ford a river in a 2WD or low-slung 4WD vehicle is asking for trouble.

Responsible and sustainable travel

Remember the fundamentals of responsible travel: don't litter, leave places better than you found them, and protect wild animals and natural flora. This applies to popular attractions such as the Golden Circle as well as the wild interior, where you are alone with the glaciers and volcanoes. Visit Nature.is for information on environmentally friendly travel in Iceland. Admire Icelanders' open-minded creativity.

Icelanders are tough, open-minded people with a dry but vibrant sense of humor. They usually speak excellent English and are up for a chat or to tell you about their favorite places to visit. Respecting local etiquette and laws (along with not complaining about the weather or how difficult it is to get to the natural wonders) will endear you to them and open doors for local connections.

They are also diverse in their interests; it appears that half of Icelanders are in a band or engaged in some form of art or craft. They're used to thinking big and having a good time. Go ahead and join them.

Consider the weather.

You may encounter bus tours and crowds of tourists in popular areas, but Icelandic weather is unpredictable no matter where you go. A sunny day can quickly turn into snow flurries, and the stakes rise even higher as you travel deeper into the wilderness. Never underestimate the weather; instead, use the Icelandic Met Office's forecasts to plan ahead.

Remove your shoes indoors

When entering a building, Icelanders frequently remove their shoes. Bring slippers or flip-flops for indoors.

Drink from the tap.

It's pure and wonderful; if you ask for bottled water, Icelanders will look at you strangely.

Chapter 10

Iceland on a Budget

Iceland can be prohibitively expensive, but with careful planning, it is possible to visit the Land of Fire and Ice without breaking the bank. Here's how to get it done.

Sights

The horizons of Iceland are dotted with volcanic peaks, gushing waterfalls spring from every crevice, and beautiful coastlines appear to lurk around every bend in the road. Despite discussions over the years about instituting a nature pass system, which would charge visitors a (small) fee to visit some of the country's natural sites, this spectacular scenery is mostly free to explore.

Some sites, however, charge parking fees. The fee varies but is usually around Ikr750 (US$6) per day for a regular private car and is used to help fund the upkeep of facilities like walking paths, restrooms, parking lots, and service centers. Some establishments have implemented a fee for restroom use of up to Ikr 200 (US$1.50).

The Ring Road, which circles Iceland, provides easy access to many of the country's major attractions. Showstoppers along the south coast include incredible waterfalls like Seljalandsfoss, where you can walk behind the falls, and Skógafoss, where rainbows arc through the spray in the sunlight. Other highlights include the dramatic black beach at Reynisfjara near Vk, the massive Vatnajökull ice cap, and the Jökulsárlón glacier lagoon, where glistening icebergs travel out to sea, occasionally resting along the black sand beach dubbed "Diamond Beach" in English.

The Golden Circle is the most popular day trip from the capital, Reykjavik. It is home to the magnificent Gullfoss waterfall; Geysir, the geyser that inspired all others; and Ingvellir, the site of the world's first parliament.

Reykjavik is an enjoyable city to explore, and some attractions, such as the must-see Hallgrmskirkja church, are free to enter (though there is a charge of Ikr1000 (US$8) to go to the top for views of the city and its rooftops). Even if you aren't attending a performance, the city's cultural center, the iconic Harpa concert hall, is worth a visit. Meanwhile, City Walk Reykjavik offers popular guided walking tours of the city with a "pay what you want" policy. Save money by walking, taking the Straetó public bus, or renting a bike (for city cycling, check out Donkey Republic's day deals).

Activities

Iceland offers incredible activities ranging from relaxing in the famous Blue Lagoon to high-octane experiences such as snowmobiling, glacier hiking, and descending into a volcano. Some can be done on your own, but you should plan carefully because Iceland's natural environment is both wild and fragile. Tour companies offer a variety of activities, some of which include seeing the sights mentioned above, but trips aren't cheap, so pick one or two that you really want to try and focus on getting the best value for your money.

If you want to go whale watching, for example, you should research the best locations throughout the country and compare tour prices. But it's also worth checking the conditions and best times to see whales; if it's not a good time of year to see them, you might want to save your money and do something else.

Consider alternatives as well. Glacier hiking trips to places like Skaftafell in the country's southeast may be out of your price range, but walking along the glacier's edge provides fantastic views for free. Similarly, while the Blue Lagoon (from ISK6990/US$54 in low season to ISK8990/US$69 in high season) isn't cheap, you can soak in one of Iceland's lesser-known geothermal hot spots for a fraction of the cost.

Transport

You can travel around Iceland by car, bus, tour group, or internal flight. In the summer, a 2WD hire car can open up much of the country as long as you stay off mountain roads, and roads are generally easy to navigate. However, with prices starting at Ikr16,000 (US$123) per day in high season (if booked well in advance) and fuel costing around Ikr240 (US$1.85) per liter, having your own wheels isn't always cheap, so weigh your options.

Avoid airport taxis to save money on travel. Keflavik International Airport is located 50 kilometers from Reykjavik. If you don't want to rent a car, take one of the airport buses, which run on a regular basis and cost INR

3300 (US$25). A large taxi may be less expensive for larger groups. The public bus Strtó also runs several times per day. It takes about 30 minutes longer but costs Ikr2000 (about $15 USD).

During peak season, reserve your rental car well in advance. Better yet, travel outside of peak season to take advantage of lower rates.

Compare tour prices in the area you want to visit with the cost of renting a car for the day. If you're traveling with a group of friends, renting a car may be the most cost-effective way to complete a route like the Golden Circle while also allowing you to explore the area at your own pace.

Use the bus. Strtó operates bus services within the capital as well as to towns throughout the country. During the summer, Reykjavik Excursions offers a bus pass to the Highlands; however, check timetables as some services run infrequently. Again, compare the cost of hiring a car, which may be less expensive than taking the bus if you are traveling with two or more people.

Although hitchhiking is never completely safe, and we do not recommend it, some people do hitchhike in Iceland. You'll need a lot of patience as well as weatherproof clothing. Alternatively, you can pre-arrange a ride using the carpooling website samferda.is. It is generally expected that you will contribute to the cost of fuel.

Even the most basic accommodation in Iceland is not cheap. Traveling outside of peak season, from June to August, usually means significantly lower accommodation prices.

How to save money on lodging: Book early, especially during peak season. Accommodation options are limited in some popular areas of the country, such as the route between Vk and Jökulsárlón.

Pack a sleeping bag. For a lower price, a few establishments provide beds without a duvet or blanket.

Before your trip, join Hostelling International to receive a discount on most hostel stays.

Camping is not only the cheapest option, but it also allows you to wake up in some of Iceland's most spectacular locations, such as in the shadow of Skógafoss waterfall. If you're traveling with a family or staying in Iceland for an extended period of time, consider purchasing the Camping Card, which provides 28 nights of access to camping spots throughout the country and may be less expensive.

Food and beverages

Food and drink can deplete your budget, but there are some simple ways to save money.

How to save money on food and drink: Stay in a place with a kitchen, buy supplies at cheaper supermarkets like Bónus and Krónan, and pack a lunch for the road.

Bring a reusable bottle and drink from the tap! Iceland has some of the cleanest water on the planet.

Buy alcohol at the airport because it is tax- and duty-free, making it much cheaper than in stores and bars.

Keep an eye out for happy hours in Reykjavik. The Reykjavik Appy Hour app can assist you with this.

Conclusion

Iceland, oh Iceland! The magical and mysterious land of lava rocks and black beaches, larger-than-life mountains, and dramatic landscapes has become a must-see destination for tourists from all over the world in recent years.

So, what's the big deal about this Nordic island country? Here are ten reasons why everyone is crazy about Iceland— and why you should go.

1. The aurora borealis is breathtaking.

Iceland is equally beautiful at night as it is during the day. The aurora borealis (or northern lights) occur all year but are only visible in clear, dark skies. You have a good chance of capturing the celestial, gorgeous green hues between 8 p.m. and 2 a.m. from September to early April.

2. In the summer, the sun never sets.

If you've ever wished for more fun in the sun, summer in Iceland is for you. Due to the tilt of the Earth's axis and Iceland's location in the Arctic Circle, the sun barely sets at midnight and rises again at 3 a.m. from mid-May to late July. The summer solstice midnight sun phenomenon is in full force on June 21, when the sun reaches its highest point in the sky.

3. You'll have a whale of a story to tell.

While looking for sea giants on Cape Cod is an exciting adventure, New England whale watching does not always produce results. You're almost certain to see at least one of the twenty indigenous species that circle the island, including minke and humpback whales. Most whale-watching excursions will also take you to seaside cliffs to see puffins, the country's adorable unofficial mascot.

4. It's ideal for weekend warriors and nature lovers.

In the Land of Ice and Fire, you can experience the best of both worlds. There are numerous glaciers and glacial lakes to explore, such as the Jökulsárlón lake in southeast Iceland, and you must visit the Rhnkaggur magma chamber, which takes you into the heart of a dormant volcano. If you're looking for a challenging workout or simply want to take the perfect Instagram photo, Iceland's many mountains are a hiker's paradise. You can choose a hike that is appropriate for your level of comfort, whether you are a novice alpinist or an experienced mountaineer.

5. You can swim in a geothermal lake.

Iceland generates electricity using geothermal energy, and natural pools can be found throughout the country, but the Blue Lagoon, a large lake on the Reykjanes peninsula with an average water temperature of 102 degrees year round, is a popular swimming destination.The warm seawater contains minerals such as silica and sulfur, which heal and rejuvenate the skin.

6. The Golden Circle is the most beautiful journey you'll ever take.

The 300-kilometer round trip, which begins and ends in the capital city of Reykjavik, will take you through the most scenic parts of Iceland in one day. Wind your way through the national park Ingvellir, the Great Geysir at Haukadalur (which only erupts a few times a year), and the rainbow-making waterfall Gullfoss. Don't forget to bring your camera; these will be the photos you frame to remember your trip to Iceland.

7. You can enjoy a different type of beach.

Iceland has beautiful black beaches, such as Reynisfjara, a black pebble beach near the southern village of Vk, known for its black basalt cliffs and massive caves, and the "Diamond Beach" of Breidamerkursandur, which is adorned with ice diamonds all year. Instead of warm weather and tropical breezes, the black beaches offer a rare type of beauty that appears only in dreams.

8. It is the friendliest country in the world.

Iceland was named the friendliest nation in 2013 by the World Economic Forum's Travel and Tourism Competitiveness Report on global tourism. Aside from plenty of transportation and attractions, the report observed the attitude of Icelandic residents, so be prepared to be welcomed with open arms by the lovely locals.

9. The food is delicious, fresh, and pure.

GMOs and artificial ingredients are less prevalent due to the Scandinavian cuisine culture of using fresh fare from the surroundings. Locals prefer Skyr, a creamy cheese-like dairy dish, but classic dishes you'll recognize include lobster, salted cod, lamb, and—surprisingly—hot dogs.

All these and more are good reasons why your next holiday stop should be Iceland.

Happy Vacation!

www.ingramcontent.com/pod-product-compliance
Lightning Source LLC
Chambersburg PA
CBHW052126150726
48002CB00006B/2495